Contents

How to Use This Book

The goal of *Comprehensive Literacy* is to increase the learners' proficiency in literacy skills at the kindergarten level. The subject matter featured in these activities has been chosen based on curriculum used in schools nationwide. The activities and skills follow a sampling of the National Council of Teachers of English (NCTE) standards with a focus on science and social studies topics. These activities have been designed to capture the learners' interests by presenting material in a fun and exciting way.

Comprehensive Literacy is organized into six sections: Phonemic Awareness, Phonics: Letter-Sounds, Vocabulary, Fluency, Understanding Fiction, and Understanding Nonfiction. Each section focuses on an important aspect of comprehensive literacy, offering easy-to-understand skill definitions and activity directions.

Phonemic Awareness
Phonemic awareness activities in this section require the learner to listen and respond orally. Learners practice hearing patterns in rhyming words and orally blending sounds to make new words.

Phonics: Letter-Sounds
In this section, learners practice connecting letters with consonant sounds and short and long vowel sounds. Recognizing the relationships between letters and sounds gives learners the ability to decode words.

Vocabulary

In this section, different categories of vocabulary words are featured, including number words, color words, naming words, and describing words. Words are paired with familiar pictures and photographs.

Fluency

Learners are encouraged to develop fluency through reading aloud sentences and stories with picture-words, repeated word patterns, and rhyming words.

Understanding Fiction

Learners examine the components of a fiction story. Exercises target ordering events, recognizing the main idea, making predictions, and answering questions about a story.

Understanding Nonfiction

Nonfiction reading is highlighted in this section as a source for information. Learners will study road signs and learn about safety. Also, learners practice reading for details, drawing conclusions, and using context clues to determine meaning.

Name _____

Animal Fun

We can learn to read by listening to the sounds at the beginnings and endings of words.

Directions: Look at the pictures in the box. Follow each direction below.

1. Put a line _____ under the picture that begins the same as *bee*.

2. Put a circle ◯ around the picture that begins the same as *dog*.

3. Put a square ☐ around the picture that ends the same as *pen*.

4. Put an X on the word that ends the same as *mat*.

Name _____

Missing Sounds

We can learn to use consonant and vowel sounds to read new words.

Directions: Fill in the missing letters in the words to name the pictures below.

1. h a _____

2. _____ o g

3. c _____ k e

4. k _____ t e

5. _____ a n

6. c _____ t

People, Places, and Things

Sentences are made up of words that tell about people, places, and things.

Directions: Circle the pictures of people.

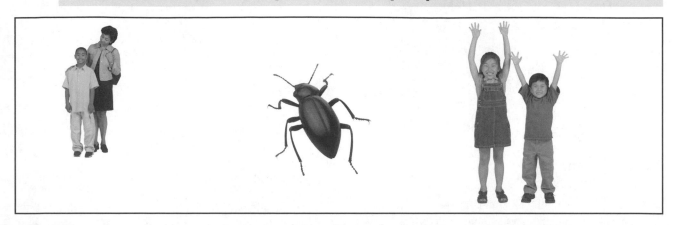

Directions: Circle the pictures of the places.

Directions: Circle the pictures of the things.

Name _____

Time to Read!

We can practice reading aloud stories that follow a familiar word pattern.

> **Directions: Listen to the story. Read the story aloud with an adult. Read the story aloud by yourself.**

Tim went to the zoo.

He saw a giraffe.   He saw a lion.   He saw a tiger.

> **Directions: Listen to the sentences. Read each sentence aloud. Circle the rhyming words in each sentence.**

The **cat** is **fat**.

Sam got **ham** and **jam**.

Name _____

Eating Breakfast

We can understand the main idea and the sequence of events in stories.

✏️ **Directions: Write 1, 2, or 3 under each picture to show what happened first, second, and third.**

✏️ **Directions: Talk about the answers to each of the questions below.**

What is this picture-story about?

What do you think will happen next?

Name _____

Apples

Words and pictures help us understand facts in stories.

✏️ **Directions: Read the story. Circle the words that describe apples. Put an X on the food we can make from apples.**

Apples grow on trees. Apples can be red, green, or

yellow. We can make pie from apples.

✏️ **Directions: Listen to the questions. Circle the picture that answers each question.**

1. Where do apples grow?

2. What can we make from apples?

9

Teaching Tips...

TEACHING TIPS

Background

• Phonemic awareness is the ability to hear individual sounds in spoken language. Understanding how these sounds blend to form words is a foundation of reading.

Homework Helper

• Say a familiar one-syllable word to the learner (i.e., *ran*, *cake*, etc.). Ask the learner to repeat the word. Say a second word with the same vowel sound. Have the learner repeat both words. Point out that both have the same vowel sound. Have the learner name another word with the same vowel sound.

Research-based Activity

• Ask the learner to choose five words in a picture dictionary that begin with the same sound and draw a picture for each word. Have the learner write the word underneath each picture and read it aloud.

Test Prep

• Learners at this level are introduced to activities that will prepare them for the testing format they will encounter on standardized tests beginning in higher elementary grades. The test preparation skills covered in this section include reading and following written directions, and selecting answers from a multiple-choice format.

Different Audiences

• To adapt this section to a special needs learner, make several flash cards of one-syllable words and their pictures (i.e., *man*, *can*, *car*, etc.). Show the learner two cards. Say the words and ask the learner to repeat them. Have the learner identify the rhyming words.

Name _____

Animal Homes

A beginning sound is the first sound we hear in a word.

> ✏️ Directions: Animals live in many kinds of places. Listen to each sentence. Follow the directions for each example. Say the names of the animals that begin with the same sound.

1. A **bear** lives in a cave. A **bird** lives in a tree. Circle the animal that begins with the same sound as **bird** and **bear**.

2. A **turkey** lives on a farm. A **tiger** lives at the zoo. Circle the animal that begins with the same sound as **turkey** and **tiger**.

3. A **cow** lives on a farm. A **camel** lives where it is hot. Circle the animal that begins with the same sound as **cow** and **camel**.

Challenge: Think of animal names that begin with the same sounds as **rat**, **mouse**, and **dog**.

11

Name _____

Going on a Trip

An ending sound is the last sound we hear in a word.

✏️ **Directions: Write the ending sound for each word.**

1. b u _____

2. c a _____

3. v a _____

✏️ **Directions: Listen to the story. Say the last sound you hear in each boldfaced word. Write the word that belongs in the last sentence.**

Jane will go on a trip.

She can ride on a **bus**.

She can ride in a **car**.

She can ride in a **van**.

Jane picked the one that ends the same as **fan**.

Jane will go in a _____ _____ _____.

Challenge: Think of two things that Jane could take with her on her trip. What are the ending sounds of these words?

12

Name _____

Time to Rhyme

Listening to rhyming words helps us to understand sounds we hear and say.

✏️ **Directions: Listen to the two words in each row. Say the words. Circle the pairs of picture-words that rhyme.**

1. can   pan

2. hen   ten   **10**

3. pin   hat

✏️ **Directions: Listen to the word on the left. Fill in the missing letters on the right to make a rhyming word. Say the words.**

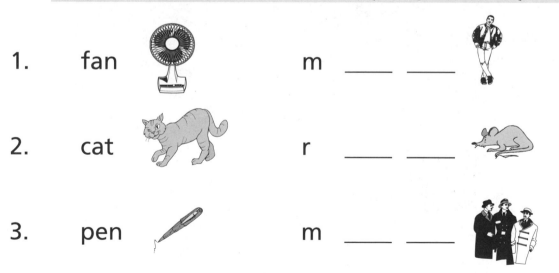

1. fan   m ___ ___

2. cat   r ___ ___

3. pen   m ___ ___

Challenge: Write the word **net** on a piece of paper. How many rhyming words can you make by changing the first letter of the word?

13

Name _____

Fun with Words

*We can put separate sounds together to make new words. In the word **man**, the sounds **m/a/n** blend together.*

Directions: Listen to each sentence. Write the letters you hear in each picture-word. Blend the sounds together to read each word.

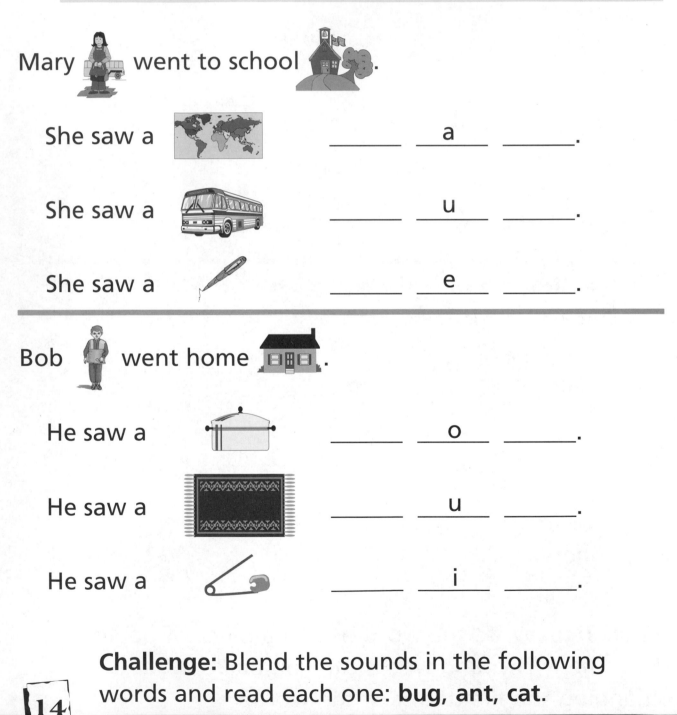

Mary ___ went to school ___.

She saw a ___. _____ a _____ _____.

She saw a ___. _____ u _____.

She saw a ___. _____ e _____.

Bob ___ went home ___.

He saw a ___. _____ o _____.

He saw a ___. _____ u _____.

He saw a ___. _____ i _____.

Challenge: Blend the sounds in the following words and read each one: **bug, ant, cat.**

Name _____

Skill Check—Phonemic Awareness

Directions: Listen to each group of words. Circle the words in each row that begin with the same sound.

bag   tub   bat

_____

cup   car   box

Directions: Listen and follow the clues to find each rhyming word. Write in the missing letter for each word.

A number that rhymes with **pen** is _____ e n.   **10**

An animal that rhymes with **wig** is _____ i g.

Directions: Look at the pictures. Listen to the words. Write the missing letters for each word. Read each word.

_____ _____ u _____

_____ o _____

TEACHING TIPS

Background

• Phonics is a method of teaching reading that focuses on the connection between written letters and their sounds.

Homework Helper

• Have learners walk around their homes or neighborhoods with a parent or guardian. Aid them in making a list of the objects they see. Guide learners in circling objects on the list that have the same beginning sounds.

Research-based Activity

• With the help of a parent or older student, have learners visit an educational Web site with pictures of animals. Ask learners to pronounce the ending sounds in four animal names. Help them write the names. Have them think of other words with the same ending sounds.

Test Prep

• Learners at this level are introduced to activities that will prepare them for the testing format they will encounter on standardized tests beginning in the higher elementary grades. The test preparation skills covered in this section include reading and following written directions, and choosing and writing the correct answers to questions.

Different Audiences

• To adapt this section to an accelerated learner, ask the learner to write two words containing each of the following short vowel sounds: **a**, **e**, **i**, **o**, and **u**. Next, ask the learner to make up five sentences, using one of the words in each sentence. Repeat the activity using long vowels.

Name _____

Winter and Summer

We can match beginning sounds to letters.

Directions: Listen to the sentences. Draw a line from each picture to its beginning letter-sound.

Pat lives in a place that is cold in the winter.
What will Pat wear when it is cold?

                                    h

                                    c

Pam lives in a place that is warm in the summer.
What will Pam see in the summer?

                                    n

                                    b

Challenge: Think of other summer and winter words.
What letter-sound does each word begin with?

Name _____

At the Store

We can match ending sounds to letters.

Directions: The pictures below show things we can buy at the store. Look at each picture. Write the ending sound for each word.

1. m o _____

2. b a _____

3. b e _____

4. p a _____

5. b o o _____

Challenge: Think of foods you buy at the store. What are their ending sounds?

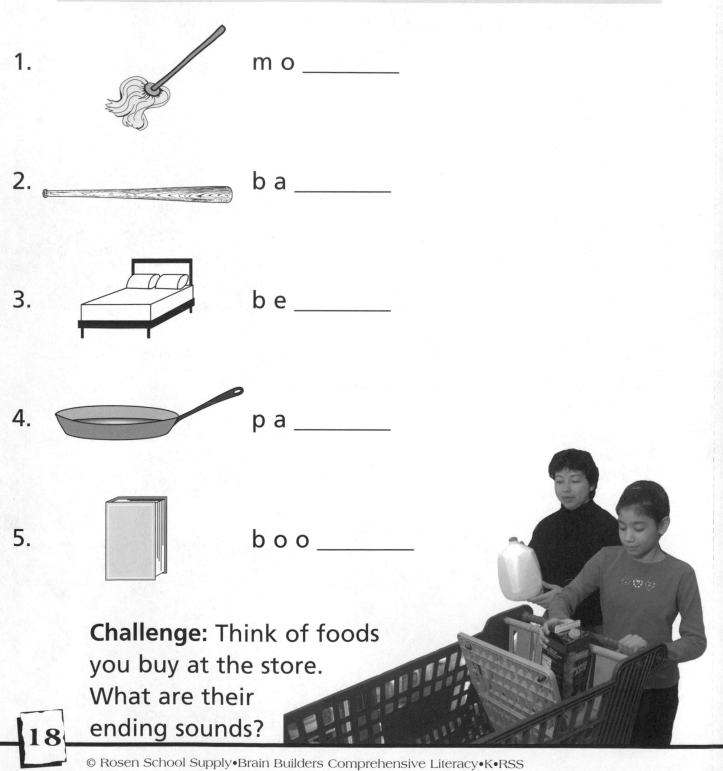

18

Name _____

Animal Names

*The letters **a**, **e**, **i**, **o**, and **u** are called vowels. We blend consonant sounds with short vowel sounds to make words.*

Directions: Read each word. Say each short vowel sound. Write the missing vowel for each animal name.

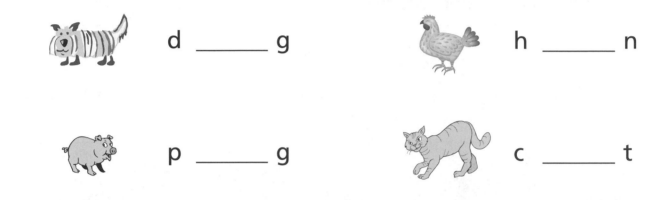

d _____ g   h _____ n

p _____ g   c _____ t

Directions: Fill in the missing letter to make a new word that rhymes with each animal name on the left.

1. hen   _____ e n

2. cat   _____ a t

3. bug   _____ u g

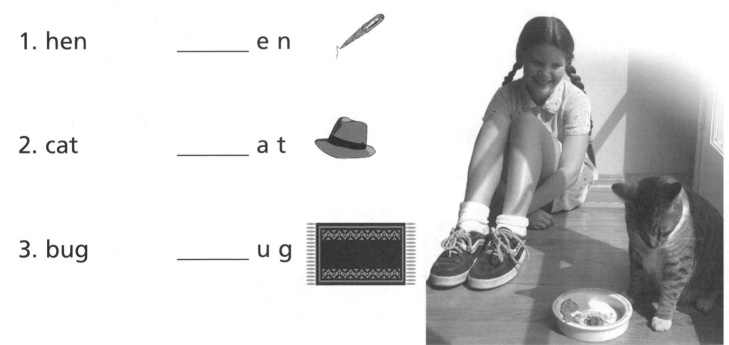

Challenge: Look at a picture book about animals. Look for words that have the same vowel sounds as **dog**, **hen**, **cat**, **pig**, and **bug**.

19

Name _____

Word Matching

*When a vowel sounds like its name, it is called a long vowel sound. Some words with long vowel sounds are spelled with silent **e** at the end.*

Directions: Circle the picture that matches each word with a long vowel sound on the left.

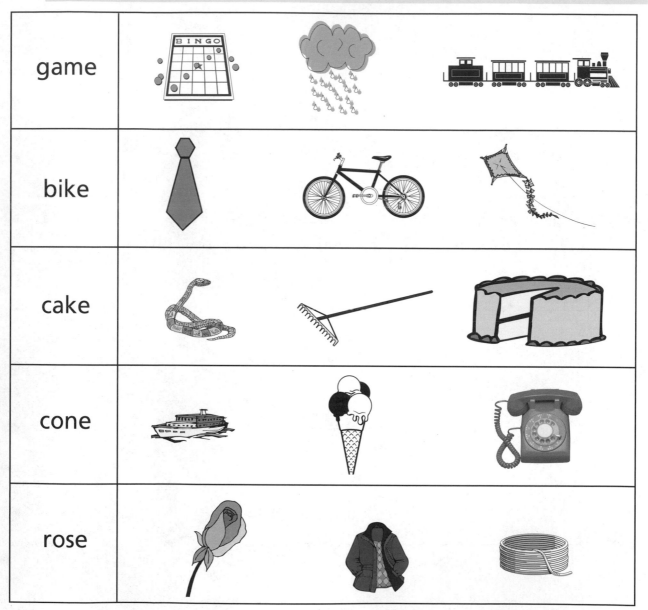

Challenge: Look in a book or picture dictionary for words that have long vowel sounds. Make a list of them.

Name _____

Skill Check—Phonics: Letter-Sounds

✏️ **Directions:** Look at the pictures of things you can find in your kitchen. Circle the word that names each picture.

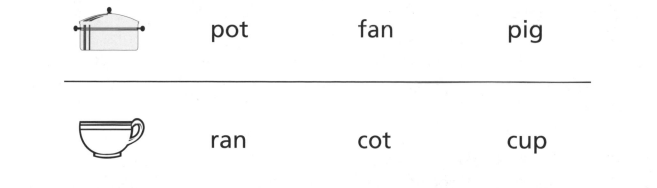

pot	fan	pig

_____

ran	cot	cup

✏️ **Directions:** Look at the pictures of things you can find in your bedroom. Say the short vowel sound for each word. Write the missing vowel in each word.

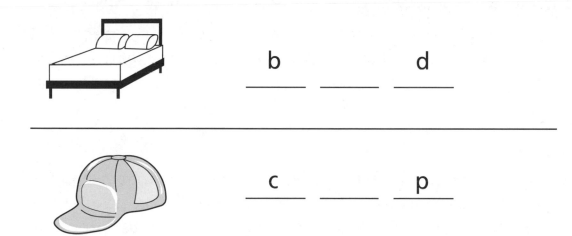

b ___   ___ d

_____

c ___   ___ p

✏️ **Directions:** Circle the picture and word that have a long vowel sound.

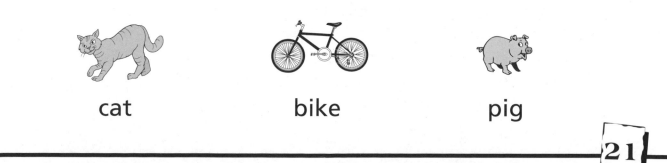

cat   bike   pig

21

Background

- At this level, vocabulary instruction includes teaching parts of speech such as nouns, verbs, and adjectives. It is also important for learners to practice reading high-frequency words such as number and color words.

Homework Helper

- Create cards to practice color words with learners. For each color, one card should show the color and one card should show the color word. Place mixed cards face up on a table. Ask learners to take turns matching the color picture card to the color word card.

Research-based Activity

- Have each learner make three columns on a piece of paper. Label the columns **person**, **place**, and **thing**. Guide each learner with using a picture dictionary to write three words for each column. Ask learners to share their findings in a large group.

Test Prep

- Learners at this level are introduced to activities that will prepare them for the testing format they will encounter on standardized tests beginning in higher elementary grades. The test preparation skills covered in this section include reading and following directions, and using pictures to understand information.

Different Audiences

- To adapt this section to ESL learners, give the learners a deck of cards with numbers and objects up to 10. For each card, ask learners to say the number in their native language. Then say the number in English and ask learners to repeat it. Repeat up to 10. Last, ask learners to say the numbers on the cards in English only.

Name _____

Counting Our Way to School

We use number words to describe how many things there are.

Directions: Read the story. Answer each question with a number word.

Rob saw many things on his way to school. He saw:

1—one

2—two

3—three

4—four

5—five

How many 🚙 did Rob see? _____

How many 📫 did Rob see? _____

How many 🚲 did Rob see? _____

How many 🚌 did Rob see? _____

Challenge: Count the number of buses you see on the way to school. Write the number word.

23

Name _____

The Colors of Food

We use color words to describe things we eat everyday.

Directions: Read the sentences. Color the pictures.

1. An 🍎 is red.

2. A 🍌 is yellow.

3. A 🥕 is orange.

4. Some 🥬 is green.

Challenge: Draw and color a picture of something you ate or drank today that is red, green, or yellow.

24

Name _____

At the Park

We can learn words that name people, places, and things.

✏️ **Directions: Use the words in the box to complete the story. Use the pictures in the story as clues. Read the story.**

dog	mom	home	park	book	tree

Joe went to the _____ with his

_____ . Joe saw a _____ .

Joe sat under a _____ and read a

_____ . Then Joe and his mom went

_____ .

Challenge: Pick one person, one place, and one thing. Make up a sentence using these words.

Name _____

Fun at the Zoo

We use describing words to tell more about a person, place, or thing.

> **Directions: Listen to each sentence about zoo animals. Circle the word that describes the animal. Write the word on the line.**

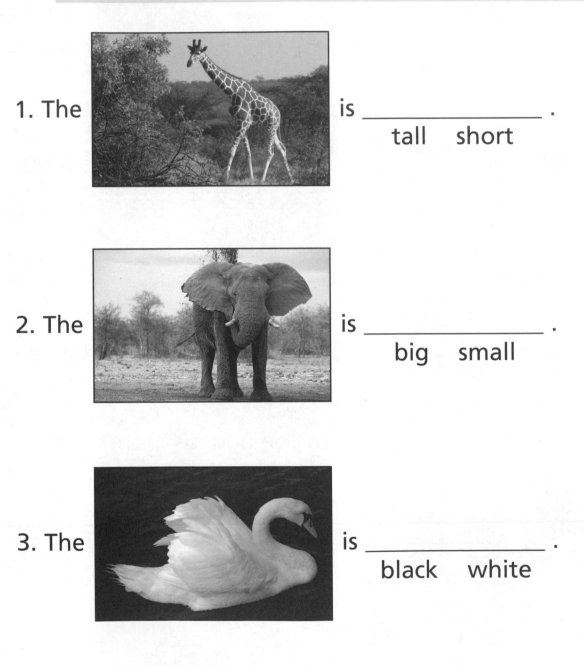

1. The [giraffe] is _____ .

   tall   short

2. The [elephant] is _____ .

   big   small

3. The [swan] is _____ .

   black   white

Challenge: Think of other animals. Write two or more words that describe them.

26

Name _____

Skill Check—Vocabulary

✏️ **Directions:** Read each sentence. Follow the directions.

Color two 📪 blue.

Color four 🚚 green.

✏️ **Directions:** Read each sentence. Put a circle around the people. Put a square around the places. Put an **X** on the things.

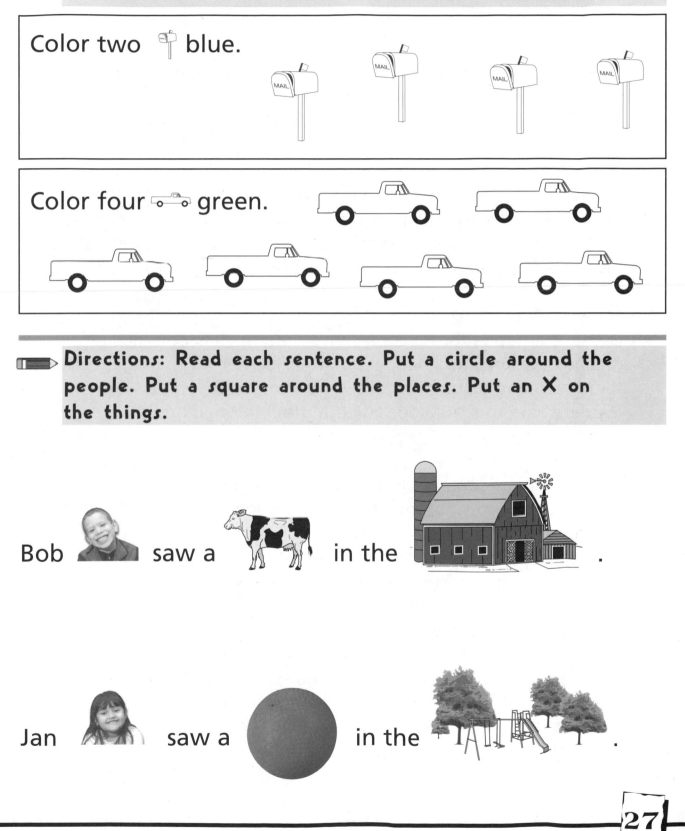

Bob ___ saw a ___ in the ___ .

Jan ___ saw a ___ in the ___ .

Teaching Tips...

Background

• The ability to read fluently is based on accuracy and oral reading ability. Learners can develop reading fluency from listening to text and from shared reading practice with a skilled reader.

Homework Helper

• Provide a four-line poem similar to those on page 32. Ask a parent or skilled reader to read the poem aloud to the learner, pointing to each word as it is spoken. Have the learner repeat the poem aloud several times. Have learners read their poems in groups.

Research-based Activity

• List several topics that are relevant to recent classroom discussion (holidays, history, addition, etc.). Guide learners in finding a book at their instructional reading level on one of these topics. Allow learners time to read aloud to each other in small groups.

Test Prep

• Learners at this level are introduced to activities that will prepare them for the testing format they will encounter on standardized tests beginning in higher elementary grades. The test preparation skills covered in this section include reading and following directions, and choosing the correct answers to questions.

Different Audiences

• To adapt this section to a special needs learner, ask the learner to pick a favorite toy or object. Have the learner make up a short sentence about the object. (For example: The boat is blue.) Assist the learner in writing the sentence using the model on page 29, building the sentence one word at a time. Have the learner read the sentence aloud.

TEACHING TIPS

Name _____

Word Boxes

Repeating word patterns can help us understand how sentences are formed.

✏️ **Directions: Listen to an adult read each group of words. Read each group of words by yourself. Color the pictures.**

1. The boat
   The boat is
   The boat is blue.

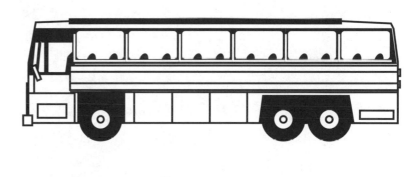

2. The bus
   The bus is
   The bus is yellow.

3. The jet
   The jet is
   The jet is red.

Challenge: Find a sentence in your favorite book. Say the first word. Then say the first two words. Add one word at a time until you have said the sentence.

29

Name _____

Rhyming Sentences

Sentences are made of words. Rhyming patterns in sentences help us read.

> **Directions:** Listen to each sentence. Read the sentence with an adult. Circle the two words that rhyme in each sentence.

1. The **dog** is near the **frog**.

2. The birds **fly** in the **sky**.

3. The **man** has a **can**.

4. The **boy** has a **toy**.

Challenge: Choose one of the sentences above. Read the sentence aloud. Draw your own picture of it.

Name _____

Taking a Trip

We can use word patterns in sentences to help us read a story.

Directions: Listen to the story. Read the story aloud with an adult. Read the story by yourself.

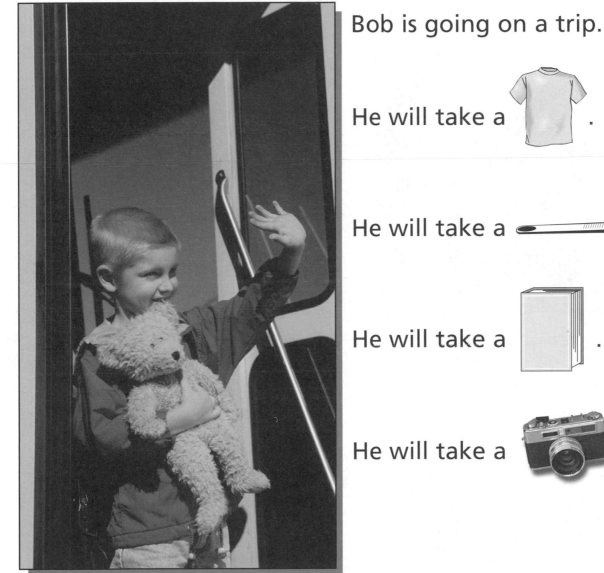

Bob is going on a trip.

He will take a  .

He will take a _____ .

He will take a _____ .

He will take a _____ .

Challenge: Make up your own story about going on a trip. Draw pictures of things you will take. Tell your story to an adult.

Name _____

Rhyming Stories

We can look for rhyming patterns as we read.

Directions: Listen to each story. Read each story aloud with an adult. Circle the rhyming words.

The Seed

Bill plants a **seed**.

What does it **need**?

It needs water and **sun**.

Planting is **fun**.

The Sky

Jan looks at the **sky**.

She sees birds **fly**.

She sees a **jet**.

She gets **wet**.

Challenge: Find a favorite nursery rhyme. Ask an adult to read the rhyme with you.

32

Name _____

Skill Check—Fluency

✏️ **Directions:** Listen to the story. Read the story aloud with an adult. Then read the story by yourself.

At the Beach

Nan is going to the beach.

She will take a ⬚.

She will take a ⬚.

She will take a ⬚.

✏️ **Directions:** Listen to the story. Read the story with an adult. Circle the rhyming words.

At the Store

Pat and Fran went to the store.

Pat got a **hat**.

Pat got a **bat**.

Fran got a **pan**.

Fran got a **fan**.

33

Teaching Tips...

TEACHING TIPS

Background

- A comprehensive literacy program helps learners understand the meaning of material. Learners study the components of fiction by sequencing events, identifying the main idea, making predictions, and answering questions about content.

Homework Helper

- After completing the activity on page 38, have learners think about a celebration they have experienced. Have them write answers to these questions: Who was at the party? Where was the party? What happened at the party?

Research-based Activity

- Read a familiar fairy tale to the learners, and discuss the events and characters. Ask learners to draw three pictures, each depicting an event in the story. Have learners trade their pictures with a partner and put the pictures in the correct order.

Test Prep

- Learners at this level are introduced to activities that will prepare them for the testing format they will encounter on standardized tests beginning in higher elementary grades. The test preparation skills covered in this section include reading and following directions, and analyzing pictures for information.

Different Audiences

- To adapt this section to accelerated learners, have the learners begin to write fiction stories about Sam or Jan on page 37. Ask learners to read their first sentence to a partner. Have the partner make a prediction about what happens next. Partners should take turns predicting and writing until their stories are complete.

34

Name _____

What Comes First?

*Looking for actions that happened **first**, **next**, and **last** in a story helps us understand the order that things happened.*

✏️ **Directions: Look at the pictures to find out what is happening in the story. Circle the answers to the questions.**

Making a Picture

Tom got paper .

Tom got crayons .

Tom drew a house .

1. What happened **first** in the story?

Tom got paper .   Tom got a book .

2. What happened **last** in the story?

Tom drew a house .   Tom drew a boat  .

Challenge: Tell what you do **first**, **next**, and **last** to make your favorite snack.

35

Name _____

What's It All About?

It is important to think about the main idea of a story as you read.

Directions: Read the picture story. Circle the answers to the questions.

Mary's Bedroom

Mary has a [bed] in her bedroom.

She has a [alarm clock] in her bedroom.

She has a [lamp] in her bedroom.

Mary looks at a [book] in her bedroom.

1. What is the story about?

   Mary's bedroom   Mary's pet

2. What does Mary do in her bedroom?

   looks at a book   plays outside

3. Which of these things was not in the story?

Challenge: Read a story with an adult. Draw a picture of what you think the story is about.

Name _____

What Happens Next?

Pictures help us figure out what will happen next in a story.

Directions: Look at each picture. Circle the sentence that tells what will happen next.

Sam will go down the hill.

Sam will go home.

Jan will go out to play.

Jan will eat.

Challenge: Read a storybook with an adult. Tell how you think the story will end.

37

Name _____

At the Party

*Good readers can answer **who**, **what**, and **where** questions about a story after they read it.*

Directions: Read the story. Circle the answer to each question.

Nan had a party. She ate cake

 at the party. She got

gifts  at the party. She

played a game BINGO at the

party. Nan had fun.

1. Who is the story about?   **Nan**   **Fran**

2. Where was Nan?   **at a party**   **at school**

3. What did Nan eat?   **cake**   **pizza**

Challenge: Read a book with an adult. Tell **who, what,** and **where** about the story.

Name _____

Skill Check—Understanding Fiction

Directions: Read the story. Look at the picture. Use the story and the picture to answer the questions. Talk about your answers.

Jen lives in a city. She walks with her mom to school. She sees a bus on the street. She sees a mailbox. She sees a cat.

1. What is the story about?

2. Where does the story take place?

3. What will happen next?

Background

• Comprehensive literacy instruction uses both nonfiction and fiction to reinforce reading comprehension skills. Skills for studying nonfiction include drawing conclusions, using context clues, and reading for information.

Homework Helper

• Assist the learner with finding a nonfiction picture book. Ask them to look at the pictures and predict what the book will be about. Read the book aloud. Ask learners to tell how their prediction matched the content of the book.

Research-based Activity

• Provide learners with an easy-to-read map. Point out important sites. Ask questions. (For example: What could you find at the aquarium? Which is closer to the water: the museum or the school?) Ask learners to work in small groups to make a map of their classroom.

Test Prep

• Learners at this level are introduced to activities that will prepare them for the testing format they will encounter on standardized tests beginning in higher elementary grades. The test preparation skills covered in this section include reading and following written directions, and using pictures for information.

Different Audiences

• To adapt this section to ESL learners, explain the meaning of each road sign on page 41. Duplicate the shape of each on a piece of paper without including words or pictures. Ask learners to pronounce the English words as they fill in each sign. Assist learners in finding information about road signs in their native lands using the Internet.

Name _____

Signs Around Us

The signs around us have different important meanings.

✏️ **Directions: Ken sees different road signs when he is in the car. Ken knows that signs help us stay safe. Draw a line from each sign on the left to the matching sign on the right. Tell what each sign means.**

Challenge: Look for a sign on your way home from school. What pictures or words are on it? What does the sign mean?

Name _____

Dinosaur Facts

Words can help us create pictures in our minds as we read stories.

Directions: Read the story. Circle the picture that matches each describing word.

Dinosaurs lived a long time ago. Some were tall .

Some were short . Some were little . Some

were big .

tall

little

Challenge: Draw a picture of a dinosaur. Then describe what your dinosaur looks like.

Name _____

A Map of My Town

We can use information from maps to help us learn about people in our community.

Directions: Look at the map. Circle the picture that answers each question.

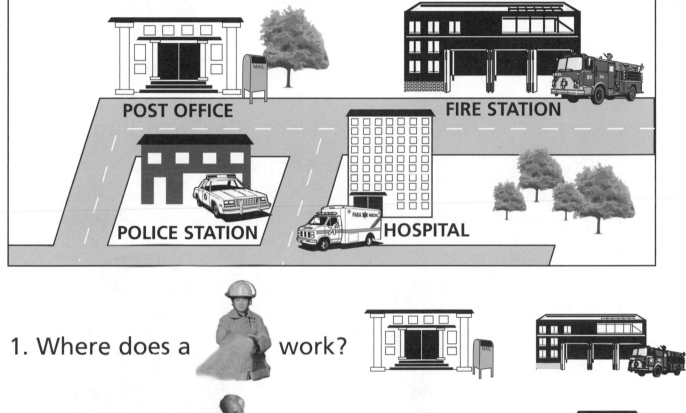

1. Where does a [firefighter] work?

2. Where does a [doctor] work?

3. Where does a [police officer] work?

Challenge: Think of a person who works at one of the places on the map. Tell what that person does to help others.

43

Name _____

Birds

We can understand the meaning of a story by using picture clues and word clues.

Directions: Use the pictures to give you clues about the words in the story. Circle the picture that answers each question.

There are many kinds of birds  . Birds have

feathers ___ to keep them warm. Birds eat bugs ___

and worms ___ .

1. What do birds have?

2. What do birds eat?

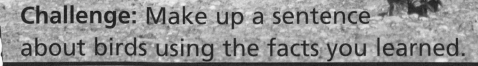

Challenge: Make up a sentence about birds using the facts you learned.

44

Name _____

Skill Check—Understanding Nonfiction

✏️ **Directions: Read the story. Fill in the missing word in each sentence.**

There are many different kinds of flags  .

Some flags have stripes  . Some flags have

stars ⭐ .

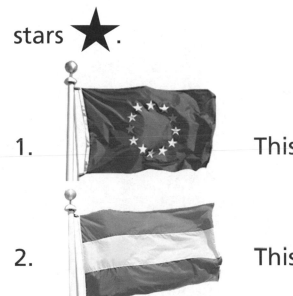

1.   This flag has _____ .

2.   This flag has _____ .

✏️ **Directions: Read the questions. Circle the answers.**

1. Which sign means that there is a school nearby?

2. Which sign means that cars can only drive one way on a street?

Answer Key

p. 4
1. A line should be under the bear.
2. A circle should be around the duck.
3. A square should be around the hen.
4. An X should be on the cat.

p. 5
1. hat
2. **d**og
3. cake
4. kite
5. **f**an
6. cat

p. 6
The people should be circled.
The places should be circled.
The things should be circled.

p. 7
The rhyming words are **cat** and **fat**.
The rhyming words are **Sam**, **ham**, and **jam**.

p. 8
3, 1, 2
The story is about a girl preparing to eat cereal.
Answers will vary.

p. 9
The words **red, green,** and **yellow** should be circled.
The word **pie** should have an X on it.
1. The picture of the tree should be circled.
2. The picture of the pie should be circled.

p. 11
1. The picture of the bee should be circled.
2. The picture of the turtle should be circled.
3. The picture of the cat should be circled.

p. 12
1. bu**s**
2. ca**r**
3. va**n**
Jane will go in a **van**.

p. 13
1. **Can** and **pan** should be circled.
2. **Hen** and **ten** should be circled.
3. **Pin** and **hat** should not be circled.
1. **m**an
2. **r**at
3. m**en**

p. 14
She saw a **map**.
She saw a **bus**.
She saw a **pen**.
He saw a **pot**.
He saw a **rug**.
He saw a **pin**.

p. 15
Bag and **bat** should be circled.
Cup and **car** should be circled.
A number that rhymes with **pen** is **t**en.
An animal that rhymes with **wig** is **p**ig.
sun
mop

p. 17
A line should connect the coat to the letter **c**.
A line should connect the hat to the letter **h**.
A line should connect the bug to the letter **b**.
A line should connect the nest to the letter **n**.

p. 18
mo**p**
ba**t**
be**d**
pa**n**
boo**k**

p. 19
do**g**
he**n**
pi**g**
ca**t**
1. **p**en
2. **h**at
3. **r**ug

p. 20
The first picture should be circled.
The second picture should be circled.
The third picture should be circled.
The second picture should be circled.
The first picture should be circled.

p. 21
Pot should be circled.
Cup should be circled.
bed
cap
Bike should be circled.

p. 23
five trucks
two mailboxes
three bikes
four buses

p. 24
Learners should follow the directions.

p. 25
Joe went to the **park** with his **mom**. Joe saw a **dog**. Joe sat under a **tree** and read a **book**. Then Joe and his mom went **home**.

p. 26
1. The giraffe is **tall**.
2. The elephant is **big**.
3. The swan is **white**.

p. 27
Two mailboxes should be colored blue.
Four trucks should be colored green.
Bob and Jan should be circled.
The barn and the park should have squares around them.
There should be Xs on the cow and the ball.

p. 29
Learners should follow the directions.

p. 30
Dog and **frog** should be circled.
Fly and **sky** should be circled.
Man and **can** should be circled.
Boy and **toy** should be circled.

p. 31
Learners should follow the directions.

p. 32
Seed, need, sun, and **fun** should be circled.
Sky, fly, jet, and **wet** should be circled.

p. 33
Pat, **hat**, and **bat** should be circled.
Fran, pan, and **fan** should be circled.

p. 35
1. Tom got paper.
2. Tom drew a house.

p. 36
1. Mary's bedroom
2. looks at a book
3. train

p. 37
Sam will go down the hill.
Jan will eat.

p. 38
1. Nan
2. at a party
3. cake

p. 39
1. The story is about Jen and her mom walking to school.
2. The story takes place in the city.
3. Answers will vary.

p. 41
Learner should follow the directions.

p.42
The first picture should be circled.
The second picture should be circled.

p. 43
1. The second picture should be circled.
2. The second picture should be circled.
3. The first picture should be circled.

p. 44
1. The first picture should be circled.
2. The second picture should be circled.

p. 45
1. This flag has **stars**.
2. This flag has **stripes**.
1. The first picture should be circled.
2. The first picture should be circled.